THE CENTER OF ATTENTION

Ron Morgan

Photographs by Pamela J

Half Full Press

Oakland, California

Design by Pamela J
Assistant Designer Nikki Thompson

Printed in Singapore

ISBN 1-887-137-23-8

FIRST EDITION

For my two favorite gardeners

Ashley who digs

and

Tom who plants

CONTENTS

Foreword

RON MORGAN is a force of nature. Anyone who has attended one of his design symposiums and witnessed his boundless enthusiasm and astounding powers of invention will certainly attest to that. But his force also lies in his ability to take the elements of nature and, magically, to transform and arrange them in ways one has never seen, or, really, even considered before.

I first encountered the whirlwind known as Ron when I was asked to lecture at the De Young Museum in San Francisco. They were sponsoring a "Bouquets To Art" Exhibition, a fund-raising event for which designers were asked to create floral arrangements inspired by works of art in the museum's collection. As I toured the exhibit, one creation clearly stood out from the rest in its brilliance and the simplicity of its execution. It was a sculptural head composed entirely of overlapping leaves by a designer named Ron Morgan. Not only had this Ron Morgan created something that was clearly a cut above the sea of container compositions that surrounded it, but the detail with which each leaf was layered and modeled was truly the work of an artist and absolutely deserving of a place in any museum.

Happily, I was introduced to Ron that evening and, true to his gregarious and generous nature, he immediately invited me to his home for dinner the following evening. As I entered his world, I was mesmerized. There were marvelous examples of Ron's wizardry at every turn, from beguiling faux finishes to the entirely innovative employment of bits of decorative detritus and familiar objects. The crowning achievement was the centerpiece for the evening: a lavish, triple-tiered epergne composed entirely of lotus leaves, holding cascades of glistening champagne grapes. Wonderful.

Ron finds his inspiration in the natural world that surrounds all of us — in the wonders and bounty of the sea, the earth, the air. But Ron's unique talent is to see what we don't. To recognize that with a push here and a tweak there, a handful of this and a sprinkling of that, plus a healthy dose of inspired talent, you can create something sublime. That's Ron's genius. And that's also what makes this book an endless source of enlightenment for anyone interested in things beautiful.

Renny Reynolds

In
The
Beginning

IMAGINE

THE

POSSIBILITIES

Versatile Assortment

Magic with One Flower

By
the
Sea

Frog Went a Courtin'

Opposites Attract

Potting Mix

Asian

Master of the Minimum

Let it Shine

Don't be Late

Fake It!

Spring Promise

Sitting
Pretty

Pull up a Chair

Basket Case

Berry Nice

Mixed Marriage

Matched

Pair

Indoor Garden

Lifting the Spirits

True Blue

Holiday Treat

Home Bodies

Object Lesson

Preserving the Past

Reflections

Sterling
Summer

GLITZ
AND
GLAMOUR

The Maximalist

What Inspires You?

A Study . . .

in Contrast

A Burst of . . .

Uncontained Exuberance

Stem
Your
Desires

East Meets West

In Living Color

Purple
Passion

Rose Garden

120

Wrap it Up!

Lemon Fresh

Wave the Flag

Color
Me
Happy

Echoes of Italy

Bred Moves

Artful Spaces

143

Suddenly Summer

Fresh Picked

A
La
Della
Rottia

Weekend Off!

Get a Whiff...

Bittersweet Memories

ENDURING

ELEGANCE

A Delicate

Balance

Color Smart

Dining Alfresco

True Inspiration

Comes Out of the Blue

Timeless

Fanfare

Sleight of Hand

Study

ENCHANTED EVENINGS

Theater of Dreams

Holiday Sophisticate

Pleasant Memories

Creative Mood

In the Company

of Friends

Past Meets Present

OVER

THE

TOP

CELEBRATING FLOWERS

My love of flowers is innate. From the earliest age, I was drawn to their infinite beauty, color and fragrance. Fortunately, my family and rural upbringing nurtured and expanded this early childhood fascination with nature, setting the stage for a life in which flowers were destined to play a major role.

As a small child, we would visit my father's aunt in the Midwest. She had the most wonderful natural garden, and I would wander for hours through the abundant rows of flowers, intrigued by the ever-replenishing rhythm of life that the garden revealed. Back home in Stockton, California, I was able to witness firsthand this cycle of life in our own garden. Guided by my father's love of creating new life and beauty, I developed a deep appreciation of nature. We planted seedlings, nourished them, watched them grow and, when the time was just right, harvested them. Those seeds that we planted together also became implanted in my life, growing with boundless enthusiasm.

My love of flowers soon expanded beyond our family gardens to the annual San Joaquin County Fair. We had a wonderful neighbor whom I would accompany each year to the fair, where she would enter the prize blooms that she had lovingly mothered to perfection. I remember being entranced by the inventive display of colors and designs, and by the creativity of the artists who were able to harness the patterns of nature's beauty, that which is so rarely appreciated in our daily lives. At the age of ten, I garnered all the courage one small boy could muster and entered an arrangement in the flower show competition myself. Fortunately for my pride, my courage and work were rewarded with a first-place ribbon. More first-place ribbons were to follow, and a lasting love affair with flowers began.

In college, my artistic nature lead me to major in the arts, and, after graduation, I briefly tried my hand as a high school art teacher. This proved an insufficient outlet for my overactive creativity, so, with the help of a family friend, I landed a highly sought-after job in London designing window displays for Harrod's Department Store. Four years later, a representative of David Jones in Australia enticed me to design their window displays in Sydney, which I did for three fabulous years. Upon returning to the San Francisco Bay Area, I opened my own wholesale shop and began doing catalog work for major department stores across the United States. As it had in London and Sydney this work involved arrangements, topiaries and wreaths created mostly with silk and dried material. After five years away from living, breathing flowers, the itch to touch fresh flowers again prompted me to open my own retail shop. Luckily, I landed on my feet in Piedmont amidst all my girl friends, and for eighteen years have loved every minute of the fun and creative whirlwind of the retail flower business.

Color is unquestionably the single most important guiding factor in my work with flowers. Everything that appeals to my senses addresses my attention to color first and design second — I eat, sleep and breathe color! The spectrum of color is what attracts us to flowers in the first place and holds our interest in them. Its incarnations are endless and inimitable. Only in nature can one find such limitless shades and hues. Color is my muse, my inspiration.

When creating a table setting, I like to make a strong statement by using one single color. I believe that focusing on one color unifies the choice of flowers, china and food. While I never want a table to appear too matched or too perfect, I feel that coordination between flowers and china makes a table setting and a meal more stimulating and, consequently, more enjoyable. The entire setting then pays homage to the glory of color by focusing on one particular shade, and, by doing so, underscores the presence of the flowers themselves, their types and their attributes beyond color. Color, while often the most striking attribute, is merely one element of a flower. By creating a piece solely of one color, viewers are asked to take a closer look at the rest of the flower. They can then fully appreciate the actual structure of the flower beyond its exterior coat of color.

Sometimes, to enhance an arrangement and make a single color even more dramatic, a punch of its complementary color will add spark. If an arrangement has little life, is dull or dark, adding a bright green or bright yellow touch, both neutral colors, will perk it up. All flowering plants have either a blue or yellow hue. When choosing flowers and foliage for indoor settings, always look for the yellow hues, which reflect light, as opposed to the blues, which absorb light. Since most flowers are placed indoors under artificial light, they need all the help they can get to look brighter and more cheerful.

Every day I receive a call — "I am having a party and need a centerpiece." My immediate response is: "What is the occasion?" From there I inquire about the time of day and nature of the occasion, and then the formality and size of the party. All these factors help determine the choice of flowers, their containers and accent pieces and, lastly, food. Everyone wants a table to stand out and to contribute to a truly memorable occasion. I am convinced that this is not difficult to accomplish. Initially, I don't worry about the design itself. What interests me most are the colors and combinations of materials. A good combination of the two naturally breeds good design.

I am particularly fond of using both homegrown and commercially-grown flowers, in addition to a large variety of produce. Produce gives strength to an arrangement which

I refer to as the "guts" — an unlikely, but appropriate, word for describing floral design. Produce is a plant's bud, foliage or seed pod, representing the beginning and end of the life cycle. Bloomed flowers represent the middle of this cycle. By combining the seed, the flower and the fruit one incorporates the full cycle of nature's beauty and magic.

The word fun should always come into play when creating a centerpiece. If you want someone to enjoy something you make, you should enjoy making it. The fun you have in the process becomes part of the centerpiece and is subsequently relayed to your guests. But whatever you do, don't make it a full-time job. Guests can always look at a centerpiece and tell if it has been "played with" too long. The poor flowers look dog-eared and tired and no longer have the life in them to show off their intrinsic beauty. The immediate impression is that the host spent too much time on the centerpiece and probably not enough time in the kitchen! My philosophy of life has always been to have fun, no matter what you are doing. This applies to flowers as well. When creating a centerpiece begins to become a hassle, give up and take your friends out for dinner!

If there is a single, lasting pearl of wisdom I would like to share, it is do not be afraid to be different. Shakespeare knew what he was talking about when he penned, "To thine own self be true." Be as whimsical as you like and make the presentation truly a reflection of yourself. Sometimes a little bit of imagination, whim and personal preference can make or, if lacking, break a centerpiece. Odd bits of color, texture and shape that are not plant material can also put your personal stamp on an arrangement, adding the critical "je ne sais quoi." That which captures your imagination is what engages you in an activity or attracts you to an object. That nugget of inspiration is likely the element that will charm your guests as well. There is nothing more flattering than to have a guest say, "The table certainly reflects Leslie's personality."

I hope that the settings presented here will inspire you to join me in celebrating flowers and imbue you with the confidence to express your own artistic inclinations and talents. There is no set formula for creating a memorable table setting — only your willingness to experiment, to be yourself, to embrace your own inventive visions and to trust those instincts. You can do it!

My life has been, and continues to be, a celebration of nature through the infinite diversity of flowers. I have worked with flowers for 40 years (please don't count backwards!) and have loved every second of my labors. Creating THE CENTER OF ATTENTION has finally given me the opportunity to share my own individual approach to floral design and my unending enthusiasm and love of flowers. I look forward to the next 40 years with great eagerness and anticipation, and foresee sharing many more books and ideas.

COMMENTARY

ON

THE

DESIGNS

IN THE BEGINNING

OVER THE TOP

Title Page   FRESH SLICE OF SUMMER

CONTAINER: Antique brass compote.

MATERIAL: Garden roses, hyacinths, viburnum, hypericum berries; cantaloupe, honeydew melons and kumquats. Rose petals between glass plates.

The combination of flowers and fruit beautifully express the life span of plant life, from bud, to flower, to fruit. Here two types of melon (sprayed with artist's fixative to deter insects) are attached to floral foam with bamboo skewers and then intermixed with a lush variety of flowers.

13   IN THE BEGINNING

CONTAINER: Antique hand-gilded cast bronze open weave basket.

MATERIAL: Lily of the valley, hosta leaves, moss; ginger and mushrooms.

In the beginning less is always more. The importance and elegance of the gilt basket are in bold contrast with the simplicity and delicacy of the flowers. The addition of a few mushrooms and some ginger adds visual flavor and spice.

A bold visual contrast to the last floral design, Over the Top, arranged in the same container.

17–19   VERSATILE ASSORTMENT

CONTAINER: Antique Chinese lacquer gong stand.

MATERIAL: Parrot feathers, hydrangea, roses, eucalyptus seed pods, hypericum, oranges, lady apples and tangerines.

The blue and orange feathers are the color cue for the plant material. A walk through the flower and produce markets gathering an unusual assortment of blue and orange elements provided the final inspiration.

20–21   MAGIC WITH ONE FLOWER

CONTAINERS: Antique Steuben glass hat display stands from the 1920s.

MATERIAL: White amaryllis bulbs.

Simple and sophisticated. The strength of single amaryllis bulbs complements and accentuates the sophisticated simplicity, and the various heights, of the clear crystal pedestal hat stands.

22–25   BY THE SEA

CONTAINER: Antique Victorian iron urns, collection of Victorian bronze statuettes and seashell grand tour souvenirs.

MATERIAL: Seashell topiaries, constructed by hot gluing seashells to styrofoam cones; collection of seashells and coral; gardenias and stephanotis.

Create a dining room seascape. The inspiration here were the scallop shell dinner plates. Shells and gardenias are freely scattered among the topiary trees, and stephanotis fills the bronze statuettes. The addition of the two flowers unifies the entire tablescape. (The shell topiaries were washed with a walnut house stain to create an antique patina.)

26–27   FROG WENT A COURTIN'

CONTAINER: Large plastic saucer with a block of flower foam stacked with giant sunflower seed heads.

MATERIAL: Frog candle, sunflower heads, water lily pods, sword fern, succulents, and anthurium foliage.

A whimsical version of a water lily pond. A charming candle frog sits amidst giant sunflower lily pads. Large green anthurium foliage on the table and ferns growing out of the illusionary pond complete the water landscape.

28–29 OPPOSITES ATTRACT

CONTAINER: Large antique Victorian fish bowl.

MATERIAL: Candle frogs, aspidistra leaves, fever-few, gladiola foliage, moss and stones.

A narrative landscape created around a pair of frog candles. Let your imagination wander freely, and we have an eyeful of an inquisitive pair of frogs, eyeing the guests from inside their glass penthouse.

30–31 POTTING MIX

CONTAINER: Antique moss covered terra cotta Italian planter.

MATERIAL: Clay flower pots, apples, lace cap hydrangea and moss.

A centerpiece for the gardening set with materials from the potting shed. The flower pots are secured to floral foam with bamboo plant stakes forced through the drainage hole. Crisp green apples complement the durable clay pots while the lace cap hydrangea adds a delicate contrast.

32–35 ASIAN CURRENT

CONTAINER: Series of clear saucers with blocks of floral foam.

MATERIAL: Porcelain Japanese koi; philodendron leaves, poppy pods, pin cushion protea, curly kale and galax leaves; black river rock.

An underwater fantasy selecting all plant material to emulate sea life. The protea are sea urchins and the poppy pods and kale are kelp. Polished black river rocks scattered about complete the underwater illusion of fish swimming in their natural habitat.

36–37 MASTER OF THE MINIMUM

CONTAINER: Flat matte black saucer.

MATERIAL: Chinese gold leaf candles; baby tears; sand, medium sized pebbles.

The candles nestled in the baby tears, sand and pebbles emulate stepping stones in a peaceful Zen garden.

38–39 LET IT SHINE

CONTAINER: Two glass souffle dishes. One 11 inch dish inside a 12 inch dish.

MATERIAL: Equisetum, zinnias, water lily seed pods, beauty berries and grass.

Soothing to the senses. Floating candles always create a mood of serenity. Here the equisetum is cut and filled between the two souffle dishes forming a self mechanic for a sparsity of flowers that allows the candlelight to shine through.

40–41 DON'T BE LATE

CONTAINER: Antique ruby red bohemian glass compote.

MATERIAL: Swiss chard, red tulips, red anemones, strawberries, leptospermum and bromeliads.

Here color is the key to inspiration with a juxtaposition of different elements. The strong contrast of the red and green in the rhubarb leaves sets the tonality for the entire arrangement. Skewered strawberries make a luscious addition.

42–45 FAKE IT!
CONTAINER: Terra cotta flower pots.
MATERIAL: Gerbera daisies; melons and a variety of cucumbers; square toothpicks.

Arizona Highways Inspiration. When the real thing is not available, use your imagination and have fun!

46–51 SITTING PRETTY
CONTAINER: Round Victorian fish bowl with pedestal base.
MATERIAL: Peonies, roses, rhododendron, tulips, viburnum; green bananas, limes and apples. Spectacular white wisteria courtesy of lady luck!

Green and white is nature's strongest and most endearing theme. Bananas, apples and limes submerged in water create the illusionary mechanics for the large lush white blossoms. The flowers are actually secured in a plastic saucer filled with floral foam that rests on top of the fish bowl.

52–53 PULL UP A CHAIR
CONTAINER: White Italian ceramic planter with arched Chinese bamboo garden stakes and small hanging glass bud vases.
MATERIAL: Garden roses, freesia, potato vine (solanum), variegated ivy and assorted foliages.

A garden on both sides of the window. The outdoor plant material is repeated inside, unifying and reflecting each other. The glass bottles tied with raffia to the bamboo arches create visual height and drama to the indoor hanging garden arrangement.

54–55 BASKET CASE
CONTAINER: Paper-mâché florist bucket.
MATERIAL: Green parrot tulips; leeks; moss; raffia and double-faced carpet tape.

The simplicity of bare essentials is always a hit. Here leeks are secured to the container with double-faced carpet tape and finished with tied raffia. A large bouquet to chartreuse green parrot tulips are then dropped in the container. The repeat of colors and textures and the unusual contrast of earthy leeks and elegant tulips make for a unique and show-stopping arrangement.

56–57 BERRY NICE
CONTAINER: Antique French white wire basket.
MATERIAL: Sweet peas, variegated ivy, barvardia; strawberries and blackberries.

Flowers and foliage are woven around the edge of the basket to create a nest for the strawberries. The red, white and green color scheme of the flowers is repeated in the porcelain and glassware.

58–59 MIXED MARRIAGE
CONTAINER: Wire tomato cage and small glass bottles secured with raffia.
MATERIAL: Roses, tulips, jasmine, camellias and hydrangea.

Nothing is impossible. Here a sophisticated hanging garden is created from a rustic wire tomato cage. The tomato cage sits on the table upside down with the prongs tied together at the top to form a cone shape. Weave the jasmine around the cage and fill the glass bottles with flowers. The result, a light and airy, fun centerpiece.

60–63 MATCHED PAIR
CONTAINER: Low terra cotta saucers and two fiberglass cherubs.
MATERIAL: Lilac, sweet peas, pink heather, parrot tulips, darwin tulips and spanish moss.

Romance is the theme here. The sweetness of the spring flowers reflects the innocence of the cherubs. The flowers, color and cherub accessories all combine to create the romantic mood for an enchanting engagement party.

64–65 INDOOR GARDEN
CONTAINER: Low painted terra cotta saucer.
MATERIAL: Fiberglass angel; succulents, freesia, honeysuckle, grasses, azalea, waxflower; sand and gravel to cover floral foam.

Bring the outside in by imitating your garden in miniature. The plant material is organized around the angel to simulate a garden setting. The theme is finished off with green leaf plates.

66–67 LIFTING THE SPIRITS
CONTAINER: Ceramic garden pots.
MATERIAL: Two miniature crab apple trees in full bloom; white polished river rock; antique Japanese figurine.

Cherry blossom festival. Our charming lady sits under one of two miniature blooming crab apple trees that in turn sit under a canopy of cherry blossoms. Enhancing and expanding an arrangement by coordinating it with garden blossoms is a wonderful way to create your own unique setting.

71–73 TRUE BLUE
CONTAINER: Collection of antique blue bottles. Blue and white Chinese compotes.
MATERIAL: Roses, tulips, hydrangea, sweet peas, calla lilies, barvardia, and scabiosa.

Various sizes and types of bottles make an interesting and imaginative collection to fill with single garden flowers of your choice. Here Chinese compotes have been used to add a variety of height and to carry out the blue and white theme; however, depending on your choice of bottles, clear cake plates could also be used.

74–75 HOLIDAY TREAT
CONTAINER: Blue and white Chinese compote.
MATERIAL: Blue spruce, paper whites; blue and white tea cups.

A pleasant break from tradition. Blue spruce, tucked into a pyramid of floral foam and stacked on a compote, creates a small holiday tree. The tea cups are filled with indoor paper white bulbs topped with moss, and then secured to the tree with wooden tongue depressors hot glued to them.

76–77 HOME BODIES
CONTAINER: Brass trough.
MATERIAL: Ming fern, star of Bethlehem, dieffenbachia foliage, feverfew, and tallow berries.

Unleash your favorite collection, and let them wander in a table garden and entertain your friends!

78–79 OBJECT LESSON
CONTAINER: Oblong brass trough.
MATERIAL: Collection of Chinese antique porcelain chickens; ming fern, star of Bethlehem, tallow berries, and dieffenbachia foliage.

Barnyard friends gathered around a garden of greenery. This table setting was inspired by the red, white and beige colors of the porcelain chickens which were repeated in the selection of the dishes.

80–81 PRESERVING THE PAST
CONTAINER: Antique hand-hammered Indian brass bowl, South American brass stirrups.
MATERIAL: Dieffenbachia leaves, calla lilies, cymbidium orchids, spotted calla foliage; brocciflower, artichokes, and pears.

A collection of antique objects makes for an out-of-the-ordinary and dramatic set of containers that display an unusual combination of plant material. Once again, floral foam is the basic mechanics.

82–83 REFLECTIONS
CONTAINER: Four tiered antique silver compote and collection of antique kutani wear bud vases and crystal candle sticks.
MATERIAL: White tulips, bear grass and variegated grass.

The use of only one kind of flower is the key to this arrangement. Single white tulips are the unifying element to the variety of other elements. The only variation given to the flowers is to turn back the petals of several tulips to add overall strength.

84–87 STERLING SUMMER
CONTAINER: Stacked antique glass cake plates.
MATERIAL: Collection of sterling silver fruit; gardenias, ivy and baby tears.

The Prince and the Pauper come to life in this combination. It is a play of elegance and earthiness, rough and smooth. The elegant sophistication and smoothness of the silver fruit and gardenias makes a successful contrast to the unsophisticated earthiness of the moss, ivy and glass table. The baby tears were freshly picked from the garden.

91–93 THE MAXIMALIST
CONTAINER: Pair of large apothecary jars.
MATERIAL: Garden roses, French tulips, iris seed pods, hypericum, peony foliage, johnson grass; pomegranates and pomegranate clusters on stem.

Everything is filled to the max! The apothecary jars, filled with pomegranates submerged in water, are overflowing with a variety of plant materials, all in shades of peach to repeat the rich hues of the pomegranates. The flowers are arranged in plastic saucers with floral foam and rest on top of the apothecary jars. When you think you're through, add two more flowers!

94–95 WHAT INSPIRES YOU?
CONTAINER: Chinese winter melons.
MATERIAL: Chinese winter melons, miniature water melons; Chinese good luck canes, dieffenbachia foliage and upright grasses; two green ceramic chickens.

Make your dinner guests green with envy without the use of a single flower! The tops of the gourds are cut and hollowed out to create containers and then stuffed with floral foam to form the mechanics to hold the plant materials. Green Italian ceramic chickens nestled among the watermelons and gourds create the world's most sophisticated barnyard!

96–99   A STUDY IN CONTRAST

CONTAINER: Rustic wood tabletop and glass cake plates.

MATERIAL: White pumpkins; gardenias, grape vines, gilded leaves; white ceramic pigeons.

Pumpkins stacked,
Pigeons nestled,
Grapevines twisted,
Gardenias plopped,
Guests dazzled.

100–101   GOLD STANDARD

CONTAINER: Antique hand-hammered brass bowl.

MATERIAL: Paperwhite bulbs, gardenias and moss; gold Venetian glass fruit.

The allure of gold bullion and the fragrance of gardenias and paperwhites make this simple arrangement intoxicatingly beautiful. The hand gold-leafing of the bulbs raises them to a standard equal to the elegant gold plates and Venetian glass fruit.

105–107   A BURST OF UNCONTAINED EXUBERANCE

CONTAINER: Antique Italian faux painted wooden urn.

MATERIAL: Roses, tulips, anemones, freesia, gerbera daisies, viburnum, protea foliage, parrot tulips, orchids; date palms, brocciflower, papaya, artichokes, bananas, asparagus and miniature watermelons.

A renaissance revival still life recreated in full contrasting colors. While most of my work follows a complementary color scheme, when I do mix color, my palette shows no restraint! The contrasting colors shown here were skillfully chosen to create this exciting combination of flowers, fruits and vegetables.

108–111   STEM YOUR DESIRES

CONTAINER: Collection of antique brass bowls and compote.

MATERIAL: Iceland poppies; lemons, limes, tangerines and kumquats.

Dine among a floating field of poppies. The weight and shine of the vibrant array of citrus fruits at the base of the containers and on the table are a wonderful grounding for the delicate and ethereal feeling of the long stemmed iceland poppies.

112–113   EAST MEETS WEST

CONTAINER: Two antique Chinese ceramic temple guards.

MATERIAL: Kale, green bananas, kiwi fruit; succulents, tallow berries, rat tail millet and variegated vine.

Let your porters carry you through a tropical fantasy. On one porter's head, a bunch of bananas forms the container, that is then filled with kale and tropical foliage. The other porter carries an arrangement of complementary foliage, set and secured in floral foam.

114–115   IN LIVING COLOR

CONTAINER: Japanese bronze hibachi.

MATERIAL: Begonias, dieffenbachia, tri-colored ivy foliage; cantaloupe, watermelon; floral foam and bamboo skewers.

Summer merry-go-round. The selection of the materials is guided by color and shape. The strong round shape of the melons and the strong round shape of the begonias, combined with a vibrant array of intense colors, become the two unifying factors.

116–119 PURPLE PASSION

CONTAINER: Iron antique French sewer drain with wooden ball feet.
MATERIAL: Clematis; Chinese eggplant, asparagus, artichoke, plums, purple grapes and beans.

Let your passion for purple run wild! Color rules the choice of elements. I gathered all things in the produce market to enhance the rich color of the clematis. All the produce is tied and skewered to floral foam with the wonderful purple clematis entwined throughout unifying all the elements.

120–121 ROSE GARDEN

CONTAINER: Antique Victorian fishbowl.
MATERIAL: Garden roses, hydrangea, polk berries, oak leaf hydrangea foliage; apples.

Summer casts her spell with the magic of lush garden roses. Hydrangea, berries, apples and colorful foliage add substance and uniqueness to the traditional bouquet.

122–123 WRAP IT UP

CONTAINER: Italian ceramic green glazed terra cotta pot.
MATERIAL: Alberta spruce topiary; green olive branches, privet berries; green apples, limes and green tomatoes.

Here a simple Alberta spruce topiary is given gutsy visual appeal by the addition of fruits and foliage wrapped to its trunk. First, using medium floral wire, the trunk is wrapped with the olive and privet branches to form a base for the fruits. The fruits are then individually threaded and attached with heavy wire to the trunk. A labor of love, but well worth the effort.

124–125 LEMON FRESH

CONTAINER: Antique Della Robbia jardiniere.
MATERIAL: Metal topiary form; lemons, grapefruit; sunflowers, calla lilies, hosta leaves, pittosporum and uwanamus.

This arrangement evokes memories of sun-drenched days by the Mediterranean. Lemons, skewered to a topiary form, complete with a grapefruit finial, emerge out of a brilliant yellow array of sunflowers and calla lilies. All work together to evoke the freshness of citrus and the brilliance of a sunny Mediterranean day. The Della Robbia container is the final touch.

126–129 WAVE THE FLAG

CONTAINER: Assortment of glass cylinders and antique glass cake plates.
MATERIAL: Roses, peonies, anemones, hydrangea, ranunculus, queen anne's lace, scabiosa; strawberries, blueberries, apples and cherries.

A red, white and blue banner setting. The containers, randomly placed on the table, are overflowing with patriotic colored fruit and flowers. Miniature flags decoratively placed between two glass plates complete the star-spangled theme.

130–133 COLOR ME HAPPY

CONTAINER: Italian wicker basket.
MATERIAL: Stargazer lilies, gerbera daisies, cluster roses, miniature red berries; watermelons.

A mouth-watering creation. The basket is filled with floral foam to establish the mechanics for the flowers. Miniature watermelons, sliced and quartered, are then stacked on top. Next the blossoms are interspersed throughout to enhance the juicy lush sweetness of the melons.

137–139 ECHOES OF ITALY
CONTAINER: Yellow French faience jardiniere.
MATERIAL: Sunflowers, dried sunflower heads, wheat; grapes, grapevines, persimmons and rosemary.

Turn your picnic into a grand affair. Majolica sunflower plates set the theme for sunflowers, grapes, wheat, persimmons, and rosemary — fresh from the fields and vineyards, still maintaining their morning blush and fragrance. You can almost taste the chianti!

140–141 BOLD MOVES
CONTAINER: Antique Japanese rosewood stand.
MATERIAL: Hydrangea, dahlias, beauty bush, red variegated tea leaves; apples.

All like elements are grouped to form individual areas of interest and are united by a uniformity of color. This type of grouping of like elements makes for a strong and bold arrangement.

142–143 ARTFUL SPACES
CONTAINER: Collection of antique iron urns.
MATERIAL: Clematis, johnson grass, moss; pillar bamboo candles.

Roadside-iana makes a grand choice. Candles are cleverly caged in wide-spaced groupings of grass that is gathered at the top to form a pyramid effect over them. Clematis is clumped at the base to add color and interest.

144–145 SUDDENLY SUMMER
CONTAINER: Large Italian wicker basket.
MATERIAL: Kale plants; red, yellow and orange large and cherry tomatoes.

First the basket is filled with kale. Then a variety of cherry tomatoes are nestled among the leaves, giving the effect of a freshly tossed summer salad.

146–147 FRESH PICKED
CONTAINER: Terra cotta saucer base.
MATERIAL: Two antique French tole dolls; miniature ficus tree, miniature daffodils; lady apples, kumquats and miniature kale.

Creating the illusion of a French country harvest scene, farmers gather nature's bounty under the shade of an apple tree. It is important that the scale of the plant material does not overshadow or overpower the figures.

148–151 A LA DELLA ROBBIA
CONTAINER: Collection of bronze urns, baskets and pedestals.
MATERIAL: Styrofoam cone and balls on stems; green apples, lady apples, kumquats, crab apples, miniature watermelons, lemon and tangerines.

Renaissance Italy comes to life in a colorful collection of topiary trees and cones constructed with an assortment of coordinated fruits.

152–153 **WEEKEND OFF**
CONTAINER: Various gourds and melons hollowed out and coated with paraffin to hold water.
MATERIAL: Dahlias, watsonia pods, cone flowers, johnson grass, hypericum berries, poplar leaves; assortment of gourds and melons.

The gourds were gathered from the market and the tops drilled with holes large enough to accommodate water tubes filled with an assortment of flowers and grasses. Leaves scattered on the table complete the autumn theme.

154–157 **GET A WHIFF OF THIS!**
CONTAINER: Table Top.
MATERIAL: Corn husks, peony foliage, bleached oak leaves, wheat, gardenias; onions, gourd and assorted breads and rolls.

A fresh and dried garland festooned down a rustic picnic table. Studded with onions, gourds and a variety of breads, the final addition of gardenias provides a surprise contrast in texture and fragrance to the arrangement.

158–161 **BITTERSWEET MEMORIES**
CONTAINER: Terra cotta saucer with floral foam.
MATERIAL: Roses, bittersweet, iris seed pods, tallow berries, maple leaves, dried sunflower heads; acorn squash and turban squash.

The bold scale and texture of the sunflowers and squash contrast with the delicacy of the roses, all encompassed by the wildness of the bittersweet. Maple leaves beneath clear glass plates complete the colorful autumn theme.

165–167 **A DELICATE BALANCE**
CONTAINER: Japanese bronze usubata and Lalique crystal glasses.
MATERIAL: White French tulips, giant sunflower heads, oak leaf hydrangea foliage; black bamboo.

Balancing the quantity and quality of the materials creates a delicate and serene sensation. Bold, earthy giant sunflower heads harmoniously combine with delicate open-petaled French tulips, all balanced by the strong horizontal bamboo. Nature adds the final unifying element — a beautiful silver gray sky.

168–169 **COLOR SMART**
CONTAINER: Rusted French metal urn.
MATERIAL: Asparagus, broccoli, curly kale; acer maple, succulents, swordfern, hydrangea; French silk ribbon.

Mauve-tipped green asparagus initiated the interesting combination of materials and colors that coordinate with, and are enhanced by, the surrounding garden colors.

170–173 **DINING ALFRESCO**
CONTAINER: Italian terra cotta urn.
MATERIAL: Green apples, olive branches, tallow berries and privet berries.

Fresh-from-the-orchard centerpiece. A topiary shaped floral foam is the base for a covering of berries and branches with a final addition of an abundance of skewered green apples. A collection of antique English candlesticks, randomly placed, adds an air of elegance.

174–177   TRUE INSPIRATION COMES OUT OF THE BLUE
CONTAINER: Green glass Italian compote.
MATERIAL: Dahlias, anemones, polk weed, oak leaf hydrangea foliage; figs, honeydew melon, Chinese winter melon and purple cabbage.

Lunch at the Villa?
Green and burgundy polk weed leads to the vibrant combination of the colors in this arrangement. One element and its colors again become the pivotal starting point for all other element choices.

178–181   TIMELESS
CONTAINER: Glass cake plate; crystal bud vases.
MATERIAL: White spray roses, poppy pods, hosta foliage, mimosa pods; brocciflower, green persimmons, oregano; artichokes and apples.

Green and white are the first and last word in elegance. Chartreuse green and white are always a wise choice for a dinner party because they both reflect light at night. The crystal bud vases are used to create artichoke candlesticks.

182–183   FANFARE
CONTAINER: Antique English brass tray.
MATERIAL: Folded and rolled sheet music; magnolia leaves, bronze celosia, hypericum; pomegranates.

A simple color scheme of copper and brown, rust and green creates a mellow theme. The addition of sheet music tucked in pomegranates raises the arrangement to a higher octave!

184–185   SLEIGHT OF HAND
CONTAINER: Eighteenth century cherub.
MATERIAL: Roses, calla lilies and cherries.

Rich ruby red and burgundy flowers echo the colors of the room decor and are repeated again in the stemware. Small scaled flowers are skillfully wired to a copper pipe that is bent to fit into the cherubs hands that creates an overall grand effect.

186–189   QUICK STUDY
CONTAINER: Table top.
MATERIAL: Red antique leather books, red coral branches, red coral beads; red tulips (with petals folded back), magnolia seed pods, begonias and pomegranates.

Pulitzer Prize-winning tablescape.
Be seated,
Open a bottle of wine,
Open a book,
Open the conversation.

193–197   THEATER OF DREAMS
CONTAINER: Pair of large pewter cherub candlesticks with silver baskets wired with twigs suspended between their backs.
MATERIAL: White tulips, paperwhites; cherries, cranberries, crab apples and strawberries.

Close your eyes, slip into the past and live the enchantment of a bygone era.

198–199 HOLIDAY SOPHISTICATE

CONTAINER: Glass cake plate and glass fish bowls.

MATERIAL: White dahlias; rock salt, candles; beer and Epsom salt.

Winter Wonderland. Snowdrifts of white dahlias are tucked into mounds of rock salt snow creating a cool winter scene bathed in the warmth of candlelight. The fishbowls have been painted with a mixture of beer and Epsom salt to create their frosted effect.

200–203 PLEASANT MEMORIES

CONTAINER: Small plastic buckets covered with stems of wheat.

MATERIAL: Dried wheat, lilies, roses, protea foliage, sorghum, privet berries; apples, olives; double-faced carpet tape, twine.

Gather together in the middle of your table several small plastic buckets wrapped in double-faced carpet tape and covered with stems of dried wheat tied with twine. Fill with fresh flowers and berries of your choice, and you have a unique and captivating centerpiece.

204–207 CREATIVE MOOD

CONTAINER: Three terra cotta saucers.

MATERIAL: Lily of the valley, dried honeysuckle vine, moss; various mushrooms.

The saucers are filled with floral foam, randomly placed in the center of the table, and then covered in moss. Next honeysuckle vine is twisted throughout, and mushrooms on bamboo skewers are added for a growing effect. Against this earthy combination fragile lily of the valley are added. The terra cotta bird casseroles nestled in moss with mushrooms carry out the theme.

208–211 IN THE COMPANY OF FRIENDS

CONTAINER: Glass cake plate

MATERIAL: Casablanca lilies, variegated aspidistra leaves, dieffenbachia foliage; rocksalt, snowball candles and large glass hurricanes.

Winter fantasy in green and white. Rocksalt gives the illusion of fresh snow that is complemented by snowball candles casting a warm glow on the entire winter scene. The rich green of the curled aspidistra leaves and dieffenbachia foliage create a beautiful contrast with the brilliant white casablanca lilies.

212–213 PAST MEETS PRESENT

CONTAINER: Large Japanese bronze vessel.

MATERIAL: Large branches of white quince; miniature antique Japanese lanterns.

The simplicity of three combined strong elements is the key to this exciting and dramatic arrangement. The strength of the beautiful bronze vessel is balanced with a profusion of white quince branches. The warm glow of candlelight from the lanterns becomes the third element that adds the final dramatic touch.

217 OVER THE TOP

CONTAINER: Antique hand-forged gilded bronze open-weave basket.

MATERIAL: Gilded bronze flowers; orchids, hydrangea, sweet peas, tulips, roses, barvardia, gold-leafed aspidistra leaves, eucalyptus pods, and grasses; antique gilded fruit at base.

The lushness of the container is rewarded with an over the top lushness of flowers. Combining the gilded metal flowers with fresh flowers and gold-leafed plant materials makes for a striking combination of complementary, yet contrasting, elements.

A Heartfelt Note of Appreciation

A most sincere thanks to all the many friends and supporters who have been involved in the process of publishing THE CENTER OF ATTENTION. First of all, to my "garden club ladies," who have encouraged me for years to put my thoughts and creations into book form. Next, to Staige, who initially got the ball rolling to publish a book. To Pamela, who has shown a willingness and eye to photograph flowers as I see them, and her remarkable ability to bring flowers to life. To Sothy, my right-hand man, who has lugged more flowers and china than he remembers or will ever admit. And to all my friends at the San Francisco Flower Market, who over the years have supplied me with their choicest blooms of the season.

And lastly, many, many heartfelt thanks to all my friends who have been so generous in opening their exceptional homes to the creations in this book: Anian, Di, Leslie, Barbara L., Sherrian, Barbara K., Betty, Barbara M., Kaye, Mary R., Katie, Marian, Kathy H., Erika, Mary W., Stephanie, Barbara R., Bunny, Kathie, Linda M., Marolyn and Lindy. Without them, this book would not exist — nor would any of the books to come.